Lethe:

a book of poetry

Constance Bacchus

Acknowledgements

The following poems have appeared in the corresponding magazines prior to this book:

'summer shirt daydream', *Hidden Channel Zine*

'tree constellations' *Them Dam Writers online*

'she' *Sobotka Literary Magazine*

'rejuvenation' and 'these vessels' *Remembered Arts Journal*

'the tree I saw while I waited' and 'fishing for bass' *Wire Harp*

'roadside stand past' *Euphony*

'coolness' *Nightingale & Sparrow*

'what if I wish for a storm' *Peregrine*

'fungi' *Silver Pinion*

'how many packs a day does that make' *Jenny Mag*

Thank you for reading my work and helping me put it out there. They all used my married name of Constance Schultz except *Silver Pinion* where my poems were published with my maiden name Connie Backus.

Also, I want to be sure to thank my beautiful daughter for listening to the same poem over and over and for asking me to read poems to her when she was 5.

And for you, my readers, thank you for reading my poetry.

Constance Bacchus

Contents

before the storm she wished for

the blue blue sky
turned

away

released
raven

wings

& winds
columbia enclosed

the dream that was

she closed her eyes
in her dream before
the dream began

she closed her eyes
& dreamt

he said

dream objects
memory fixed

dream day w/silver
shadow reminiscent of lavender

but when she
opened up he didn't

dream
faded
eyes
closed

ceres is daydreaming again

she watches from a stalled cloud
below as people dance
she's close

lithe

graceful

of the people, she's alone
will bring spring in pink, summer in yellows
she glides & her very feet
are music

she is the reason & watching
waters, mother on vacation

she glances sideways at the mountain, flirting
even helen has paused
for humans not daring to move as she climbs

& gives wings to rise a little higher

sees lovely mauve eyes
ruby lips
sunkissed freckles & she sighs

hazy summer

pine needles
& heat

camp

or woods in
the mountains

where we saw
swans once

& slept in
cabins

in between when I look
at you & when I respond

this water
is smooth

waves long
& languid

squeak squeak squeak
lake-looking swing

& birds
think they are the only ones

all the people in   town
know it's a secret

& it might seem
they sigh a lot
& don't even realize

they might wish
they could paint
the covered area of a sun-drenched dock

the way the waves are moving
the sweet geese noise

& that soft far away
answering honk

summer shirt daydream

the incipient sun is beginning
   to get warm
   hot enough
to not complain
   yet
beginning to burn
clouds on the edges

   did you know
there are different types
of shirts for summer
for heat yes
forplaceswhereitis
warm
hotwherepeople
musthavea/c

elastic tube tops roll
down when you dance
go with flip-flops
you never see
the rest
of the year and halters
cover less

on beaches
in pools
built by lakes

poolsbuiltbylakes
bylakes
poolsbylakes

deep and aquamarine
and cool in the heat until sunburn arrives at the party then every-
one feels sick

simple

our paths cross & cross
you smile//maybe wave//&

do you know I see you side
ways/ I see you in the

section where I put you
& it's not always all/

the way visible to me

I put//you//in a part I
can work w/unemotional

& yet they flow & I
do//see you//there;& if

I let myself look complete.

would not be able to
unsee & do you want
to take that chance

tree constellations

the sharp long shadow
of the sunburnt maple tree
cuts through grass
falls into
the concrete driveway
straight and sharp
with speckled shadows
of leaves spread
across in a galaxy
on the yard

he said

describe the way/geese
you want/float on the water on
the lake

peace:

a reservoir/in rancid desert

in/a puddle of sunshine
disappearing
shade/&

the only sound
from the run/

trying to look past

in a paired lawn chair
watching sprinklers

thinking of mowing
hearing a plane

fly overhead it's
sunday & almost summer&

soon neighbors will come out
to bake & water

their own &

——/

yes
I'm watering weeds

planting in sand
& you don't approve

look

——/

at the sprinkler
a certain way/
no water comes out

the plane keeps flying
& I wonder if it is

tempting a fire somewhere

the beach

your eyes flirt soft
gaze open full

of promises & then
I'm wondering

again where you are
all day & am drawn

into your dream &you,
you,

probably don't
think about breath on the neck

taken for granted & the chair
beside me waiting & how

long or what is it waiting
for only wind & ravens know

oh

& odd trees
on the south side

of the lake
stand still

& watch
wildlife poised

& wait
for children & fishers & hunters & dogs
& all the birds of the canyon

greenhouse

on a pool in the boulevard
slivers of sage

swept by wind down
gutters grass clippings

hold,hold

preordained storms flip soft
in pallet walls where chickens
scratch

a local science green carbon
absorption of warm influence

metamorphosis photosynthesis

an equation
a call

of wooden bones all
the rain, the soil, the sun

carbon-14 thoughts

of brighter green burnt
summer sienna

a city specific

sidewalk framed streets
train passes at 3am
know when it's quiet

the library charges
an annual fee to join

there's a farmer's market
if you get up early enough

& a co-op

grocery stores been there
since dinosaur times
w/prices from the future
the bank is across the parking lot

& there's a river

she

you can have all
the reason you want
it won't stop
how you feel

someone's flirting
and all she can think of
are green apples
in his orchard
abandoned at harvest

vinegar scent
xanthous leaves
carpet between
     seasons

air crisp Halloween weather
snow almost
yes snow
it is cold like that
can almost slice the air
with a warm butter knife

smell of green apples
green apples in his orchard

fish were tossed careless by the fence
they refuse to smell anymore
but the apples-

-nose candy if you walk by there

crazy fools

she wants him to take her
for a ride down the
canyon during a storm

& I bet you think I
am she & you are he &

it's a storm coming we are

in a storm & thunder allowed
out unabridged, rain has

brought that dry ground
smell & I see you looking

at me pretending you don't

& you do &
I do & I do

& I do &

it blows

rejuvenation

leaving
without looking
back

on water
close
to a river
on the sand
recline

not a ferry
line
but riding
quiet

someplace new
as if you
are 13 again
and it is
summer

these vessels

these vessels
imperfect

lifting out
rising
clouds floating

not heavy
or achy
blind
deaf

sprinkled
with modest rain

the tree I saw
while I waited

that tree keeps dancing with a
slight breeze moving every

single pine needle & who
knew pine needles could look

like they flow like they
are sweet sugar ice stuck

on a tree & I wish I could
capture the look of that

nature before it grows
too dark

roadside stand past

& the silver moon
glass circles

lit from behind
cut sharp long shadows

& taffy clouds
cross the parking lot

spiral out

spread by currents
of real oriental red rugs

& dreams

with teeth
dance in the rain

dreams with apples
on low trees

unpredictable

trees to climb
don't look

& bing cherries burst
in Idaho hot summer

coolness

heat she said *I'm hot*

& everyone needs to just cool
down in a lake

on volcanic rock cooled into a smooth

chair in all that soft sand they need to cool

their cores no shoes/get away/ dunk
your hair/pause cool

look at all the cooled blues/
the hues the skies same

as on the other side
cooling & for good-

ness sake don't look
at your cool cool cool phone & when

you come out everyone/will still be cool

as hot as it was look
out for sand

hornets & cactus hiding
in disreputable places

aware you are cool in just a swimsuit &
can burn aware of cool/it is likely

& cool you are/ so cool &

still sweat drips/all the people cool every one
glows cooly but now you can just close
your eyes & feel cool water of the lake
see the sky watch out for cactus uncool & think

how nice the a/c feels as you walk through

sublime allusions

culminating ancestral

atrocious celebration
divine divine

guess

dream 78

botulism blue
sky already
an ugly black leg

in her bow

& no matter
how bright

it's still
dark

still dark;still dark;

blue dark as night
can be & still
produces shadows

& it stretches it &

as it moves the stars
glow brighter though

distant still
there

they call *diana*

& she nocks/

she rocks/
she holds

the *arrow* the

dirty leg in her bow
& she lets it

fly free

o darwin come quick

in the room that is
outside my garden

I waver, I whisper
to small birds
& wonder

if obvious hallucinations
atrocious transformations
have weakened mother nature

set upon themselves
like wolves starving
in tundra

they set up
spectacles
beside,unmindful

they set
spectacles
on a table

of what was/
will be

set
spectacular
sunsets

gifts like
rainbow
promises

& universal
 en el aire

& all the chemicals
flying through
remain,unaware

dream 732

crash of the ocean no water in sight
in waves in waves

you are over me
you make my skin

the water the rocks
colorful fish flowing free

& the sky water the same

blue & the sky & the sky
the sky & you

syrup sweetly burns

questions people never ask
& think they know

truth the gossip drunk
talk on Friday night

w/all the potential

sleep,sleep

about the view
between
leaves

people pay for views
open on rocks

where wind glides
& lightning cracks

easily

no spaces no breath
no question what

& air dirty frightens truth

lights on the dam from the overlook

for Gary

getting darker
air guitar

blinking
row of lights

reflecting clouds
waiting

on the road it starts &

if it were a toy
the moon

down glory
days will

compete w/all

clap

watching
comes out of light

satellite star
music

symbiotic
grand coulee

pencil line
red lights full

moon arrives
bright on cue

watch out when you drive away

…& everyone should
see the full moon in
grand coulee sitting just
above the dam within reach

should feel it deep
eyes dark

werewolf night
cougar rocks

…& car lights
flash a warning
twice
on that old twisty road
steep sides
from the overlook

leave in
blinded
black/black

what if I wish for a storm

what if I wish
and the sky so large
as it is on this side-

the sky storms
with grey and purple
and scatters of blue

light streaking through a painting
from the Hudson River School
perhaps wind over gold sand
lonely main illumination

what storm isn't
     and the rain
     and the rain (listen to the rain)
the desert torrent
charging upon us
cleansing-I like the wind best-
and water on dry earth perfume

making a person
breath deep to catch some
it only smells like that sometimes
above snakes and wildflowers
over alkaline waters
through a canyon

wind that screams in caves
while fish jump on the way to the dam

canyon

space;is not
inclined
/heat/
soft hills & cliffs

you can't run up
just air/just water

I dream es morado
less blue es
verde amarillo y
lose azules of the lake

you can't drink
you can't imagine

the side you can't
keep traveling that way

siempre

the sky is overcast,unsure

the children are the first
to know. everyone else has
slept in

this is the third time she's
going around hanging off of
raspy concrete

to no particular place

looking for them
dancing w/them

in a portage of pioneers & pilgrims,
one points to another,

it storms
they find what
they were looking for

w/curtains closed
there is no storm

a woman comes back
up the road w/a bag

still as if there's no wind
still tall still
hooded

who does she think
she's fooling & what
do you think's in
the bag

a woman walked
tall w/a hood up &
walked as if she

didn't know as she blew
out smoke in the late

night windy air as if
she didn't notice it did
not stop the trees

the tree spirits are having
a party tonight all up & down
the avenue

when we pray for rain

it rains
on banks lake

forms lines
in the water

single drops
large & wet

soothing

occasional

splat!

music

fungi

if we must have fairy circles
give them peals of wedding bells
stop

wedding mushrooms wedding
vows oaths explanatory phrases

& they don't promise marriage
from an old maple

you don't care close you
are so mad at the rain in the lake

enough w/feelings enough
circles of greyish day

how about that how
about crying rings
as a sign of commitment

circles of hollow
on the ocean walk

how about too much before
over & over

the same kind of what happens
give me a hidden tree umbrellaed

& I'll see the allergies
in a forest of fairy circles

if it still feels if
it still smells sweet
what about circles

celestial prelude

pianos in snow & a small
pond frozen w/clarinets
melted & violins aching

piano trees w/blue sheets
guitar ice numbed

pianos numb

violins forgetting pianos
pianos forget it's cold

sheet music & was that all

bass sheets/pillows
would be nice
a snow sheet is not
a musty camping pillow

covered sheet music
forest dreams

in winter wishes
in alaskan dreams
w/heavy igloos

sheet music tiptoes
is cold & shakes
stays there & the floor

until spring forgets
all the blankets

when you go
back to see

cielo

it's still dark out although
the bus has arrived already

they made it sound like another planet

white on clouds might fall through
the floor w/o wings

this place in the sky where everything
is beautiful unless you trip

off the ceiling

will you believe it
do you care

I can see how this would look

do you want to be
serious as solidified lava
under a full moon

storm of july

ponderous grey over white
over blue hot sticky
sweating,sweating

go

ospreys call grey through
this cielo with cooler weather

drops loud
slap arms slap hair

absorbs
swings back

an angrier speed tastes
of swampy fenland

ozone extra ion aroma in towers
clean,clean
unbottled haze

banks lake could be another ocean on rough days

the water again waves unbelievably
blue & you know the banshees
are loose on the canal, released,

riding the wind dancing &
changing dresses again a
deeper blue grey deeper ebony

sky reflects deeper waves rush
white capped & wish of what will be, been cast past the logs in
the water again

fishing for bass

sunlight pushes behind
the coulee wall

belies the chilled air
occasionally blinds after

shadows bemoan spring

& music thrums through
fingers hours later in

the blood it pounds it
pounds & I can

still feel the storm on
the water & calming
ice snow rain

we claim shade

brought the other chair out
set it up
ready for the wind

& there you are
smelling of water

on dry earth

across my arms
there you are

a robin comes close
tugs for worms

another scrabbles

concrete & maple

it turns up
away from all the
thick scattered wet leaves

layered beneath in reds
& reds as a large truck drives by
& it rarely happens that way

It is quiet.

except those very leaves
rough concrete linking
tarred street to sidewalk

should you sweep the
leaves you should you

reveal lines creating the walk

uncover

then curb
slope bringing
unexpected birds

how many packs a day does that make

traces of fires of all the words
here and there unspoken
where dry sage burns right now
golden grass beautiful
complete logical

summer refuse to say it sleepy
   summer foreign in the mouth
        summer   wishful thinking

wish on smoke for summer on the beach
candles homemade in shells
   seaglass
blue wax candles of oyster shell and clam
and air from an ocean

smoke of fires in fields compose a haiku
permeates invasive toxicity   forget
far and wide   what to say

and imagine chickens now   magic
a beach little house tired and dreamy
apple tree and compost pile drive
and sunsets to write about   and drive
places to run until problems are too tired to be

think and then shiver think again
I love you and them and us and it's a kiss

sunlight in smoke

the light on the
grass
enters through
trees

reflects orange
looks like dry
grass

yellow orange
gold light
light

'cept where the
sprinkler is on
there it is
green yellow

the light
paints bark on
the same tree

& someday I
will know
it's name

trees & sage burn in summer

& the water that I always want
to write about can't smell the fish
but it's smooth

& smoke has almost uncovered
coulee walls
can see across the lake now

& breathe in through the nose
that smell of water & cool air

& still feel like you want
to cryyou do that

& light of the motel sign
shines as bright as that sun
behind grey clouds has been

& we are all crying now

& the moon didn't rise
above the coulee walls it was just
there from when it wasn't

& music is coming
from someone w/a real guitar
& it's beautiful

& we are all crying in smoky haze

instead of a cigarette
she just has her thoughts

why do I always feel
we will fall
into the dam canyon

when it storms
the wind blows
& the spirit

sounds like wind in the lake
calling
until a person
has to answer

people drive through

w/the top down radio
up kissing

at each

stop.

enjoy the new view
as they drive through

as they do they
can see it the portal

between walls so sexually
natural they can
see the birthing

can see that other world
just over there

& yes for me there are
always ravens for you

the coyote & for all
of us the

wind & bright bright
hot desert sun

on a swing at dusk

she looks at the dock while she swings
& the water

& she swings it away til she's empty

quiet
listen in dark

cars drive past

& maybe they'll play the music some more

www.ingramcontent.com/pod-product-compliance
Lightning Source LLC
Chambersburg PA
CBHW051827130726

47987CB00003B/1443